I0845168

Willow

C. K. Adas

ISBN-13: 9798638527990

DEDICATION

This book is for my family.

Once there was a tree named Willow that had a lot of branches and leaves.

Willow saw his friend with just a little bit
of branches and leaves.

He wanted to be like his friend.

One day he saw a woodcutter.

Willow had seen the woodcutter cutting tree branches but did not know the woodcutter also cut the tree down.

He asked the woodcutter, "Will you cut me?"

The woodcutter explained to him, "I only cut trees that are good for houses."

Willow did not understand. Willow did not know what houses were.

He asked the woodcutter to explain. The woodcutter said, "Houses need very strong trees so that they can protect people inside."

Willow said, "I am very strong! You can cut me."

The woodcutter was not sure but agreed.

The woodcutter started to cut the very long branches off Willow so that he could be closer to Willow's bark.

Willow was so happy.

Willow said, "Thank you so much I have always wanted my branches cut!"

When the woodcutter finished trimming the long branches off of Willow he got his big ax to start to chop Willow's bark.

He started to cry. Why was the woodcutter hurting his bark? "Mr. Woodcutter," he sniffed "that really hurts, why did you swing your ax at my bark? I thought you were just trimming my branches?"

The woodcutter replied, "You told me to cut you, I thought you wanted me to cut you to make a house?"

Then Willow realized the woodcutter's job was to cut all of him down. "Mr. Woodcutter, PLEASE don't cut me down. I just wanted my branches trimmed. I thought my branches were enough for a house."

Then Willow realized his tree friend was not there anymore. He asked the woodcutter, "Did you cut my tree friend down?"

"Yes," replied the woodcutter.

"Why?" asked Willow.

"Your friend was an Oak tree, they are very strong trees used for making strong houses. You are a Willow tree nice for shade on a sunny day. This is why you grow long, long branches that hang low."

Then Willow could not stop crying over losing his friend. He started to make a river of tears in the grass.

"Willow", the woodcutter said, "Please don't cry anymore. I will not cut you down."

"My friend is gone!" sobbed Willow.

"I have a seed from your friend. I will plant it close to you so that you will not be alone. Whenever we cut a tree down we plant a seed so that the earth will always have trees."

"Really?" Willow said quietly.

"Yes," said the woodcutter and he planted the seed close to Willow using some of the water from Willow's river of tears.

Willow was happy again.

The End

That is why, to this day, Willow trees are called Weeping Willows because of all of the tears that Willow cried that day.